PASSOVER
Around the
World

by Tami Lehman-Wilzig
illustrations by Elizabeth Wolf

KAR-BEN
PUBLISHING

This book is dedicated to my late father, Dr. Emil Lehman, z"l, who excelled in sparking interest in the Passover seder year after year, with a different program connecting the Exodus to contemporary life. We all try to follow in his footsteps, but none of us manages to fill his shoes.

I want to thank Judye Groner and Madeline Wikler for putting me on an eye-opening journey of Passover rituals. Thanks also to Aviva Aveira, Noa Avishai, Nurit Band, Dina Ben-Efraim, Nitza Dori, Eran Harduff, Karen Jakobsen, Edna Keshet, Menahem Pariente, Yonatan Peretz, Rachel Roby, and Yaffa Somech for sharing their knowledge with me.

Recipes for Egg Soup and Matzah Brei from *Tasty Bible Stories* (Kar-Ben) © 2003 by Tami Lehman-Wilzig

Text copyright © 2007 by Tami Lehman-Wilzig
Illustrations copyright © 2007 by Elizabeth Wolf

Kar-Ben Publishing, Inc.
A division of Lerner Publishing Group, Inc.
241 First Avenue North
Minneapolis, Minnesota 55401 U.S.A.
800-4KARBEN

Website address: www.karben.com

Library of Congress Cataloging-in-Publication Data

Lehman-Wilzig, Tami.
    Passover Around the World/by Tami Lehman-Wilzig ; illustrations by Elizabeth Wolf.
      p. cm.
    ISBN-13: 978-1-58013-213-8 (lib. bdg. : alk. paper)
    ISBN-10: 1-58013-213-8 (lib. bdg. : alk. paper)
    1. Passover—customs and practices—Juvenile literature. 1. Wolf, Elizabeth. 11. Title.
BM695.P35L365 2007
296.4'3709—dc22   2005035987

Manufactured in the United States of America
2 3 4 5 6 7 — DP — 12 11 10 09 08 07

Contents

Dear Reader,

When I was a little girl, my father began a tradition of bringing home people from synagogue who didn't have a place to go for the seder. The first time, he came through our front door with three young men who had recently arrived from Iran. When we read the portion of the Haggadah beginning with the words "Ha lachma anya" ("This is the bread of poverty") they stood up. Thinking that they wanted to leave, my father explained that the seder was not over. Laughing, they answered, "We know. We're just continuing the tradition we had in Iran. We stand as though we're ready to leave Egypt, just like the Hebrew slaves."

The next year, my father came home with a Jewish man from Ethiopia. When it came time for the main course, my mother brought out a huge silver platter of sliced turkey. He looked at her and asked: "Is this meat from the lamb you sacrificed this morning?" When she told him no, he refused to eat the meat. Once again, we learned about another tradition from a foreign land.

Ever since, I have found it intriguing that each year, on the eve of the 15th day of the Hebrew month of Nisan – when Jews around the world gather to celebrate Passover – the story is always the same, yet the customs differ from country to country.

This book will open your eyes to new places and faces across the globe and introduce you to different ways of celebrating Passover. You can adopt the customs that you like and turn your seder into an unforgettable experience.

Tami Lehman-Wilzig
Petach Tikva, Israel

Passover: A Celebration of Freedom

Passover began more than three thousand years ago, when Moses discovered his Israelite roots and developed a special relationship with God. Moses was a man of few words. He even had a stutter. With God as his coach and his brother Aaron as his mouthpiece, Moses learned how to become a leader. His goal was to free the Hebrew slaves. The strategy—developed by God—was to hit Egypt with plague after plague, until its ruler Pharaoh finally gave up and let the Hebrews go.

Moses warned Pharaoh, one plague at a time. Unfortunately, Pharaoh was a very stubborn man, his heart hardening after each plague. Finally, the tenth plague moved Pharaoh. It is this plague that provided the holiday with the name Passover. Under this plague, the firstborn boy in every Egyptian home was killed.

To make sure that the Hebrew slaves would not be affected, Moses told them to smear the blood of a lamb on their doorposts. That way, God would "pass over" their homes. Devastated by this plague, Pharaoh finally released the Children of Israel. Free at last, they crossed the Sea of Reeds and began their journey into nationhood.

The Seder Table

Regardless of the country your ancestors came from, or what country you may be visiting, the seder table will seem familiar. That's because on every seder table you will find:

A Seder Plate which is the centerpiece of the table. Its symbolic foods represent aspects of the story of Passover:

- **Charoset—Mixture of apples, nuts, and wine** (and/or figs, dates, bananas, and honey in Sephardic traditions) represents the mortar the Jewish slaves used to build palaces for the Egyptian rulers.

- **Zero'a—Shankbone** symbolizes the strong arm of God, as well as the lamb sacrificed on Passover during the days of the Holy Temple.

- **Beitzah—Egg** represents the traditional holiday sacrifice during the time of the Temple. Some say the egg is also a symbol of mourning for the destruction of the two Temples.

- **Karpas—Vegetable** (parsley, celery, radish, or potato) stands for spring. It is dipped in salt water or vinegar, which represents the tears of the Hebrew slaves.

- **Maror—Bitter Herb** (often horseradish) stands for the hard life of the Israelite slaves.

- **Chazeret**—Some seder plates have room for a second Bitter Herb (romaine lettuce is often used) to emphasize the bitter life of the slaves.

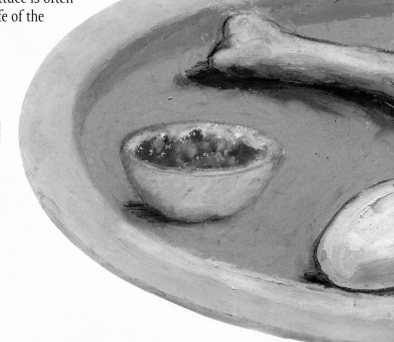

A Wine Glass for each participant. The Haggadah instructs us to drink four cups of wine (or grape juice) during the seder.

A Haggadah for each participant. The term Haggadah comes from the Hebrew word *l'hagid—to tell*. The Haggadah is the book that tells the story of Passover.

Elijah's Cup, filled with wine and placed in the center of the table, is ready for the Prophet Elijah, who is said to visit each seder as a symbol of the modest traveler who represents all people—rich and poor.

Matzah, the world's first "fast food," reminds us how quickly the Children of Israel had to leave Egypt in order to gain their freedom. With the little time they had, they baked this flat bread whose dough does not rise.

The customs associated with these objects are what make Passover celebrations in each country unique. The seder is, after all, a live, interactive play that we perform every year.

Each of us has a role on the Passover stage. We prepare for it. We gather the props, set the atmosphere, and enjoy the sights, sounds, and aromas associated with the celebration.

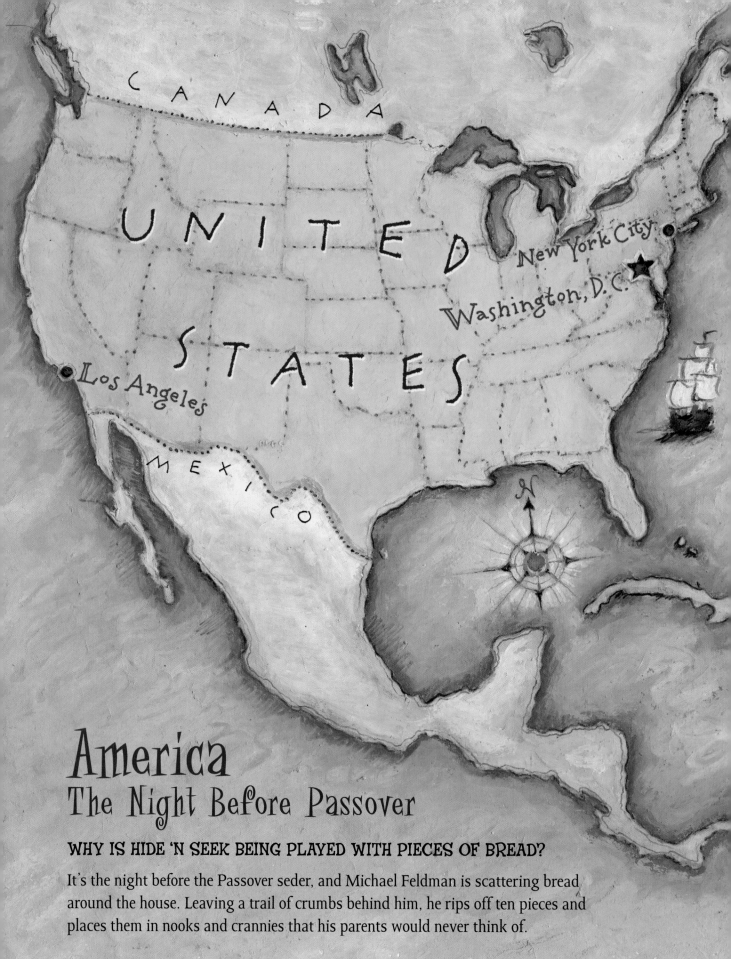

America
The Night Before Passover

WHY IS HIDE 'N SEEK BEING PLAYED WITH PIECES OF BREAD?

It's the night before the Passover seder, and Michael Feldman is scattering bread around the house. Leaving a trail of crumbs behind him, he rips off ten pieces and places them in nooks and crannies that his parents would never think of.

"Mom," he calls out when he's finished, "we're going to need a pretty tall candle tonight. It could take a long time."

The Search for Chametz—food made from fermented grain, such as wheat, rye, barley and oats—is the finishing touch to cleaning the house for Passover.

Michael's grandmother has told Michael and his sister Jessica how her family observed this ritual in their native Poland. "I had the job of placing the bread around the house," she explained, adding with a laugh, "I always made sure to hide some in the bedroom. We were never allowed to eat there, so it was my way of breaking the rule."

"How did your father find the bread if it was hidden?" asked Jessica.

"I was his guide," their grandmother explained. "I walked by his side, hinting if he was close or not." From that day on Michael and Jessica gave the tradition a name: Bubbe Olga's Hide 'n Seek.

Jewish life in America began in 1654, when a small group of Jews from Recife, Brazil, landed in New Amsterdam. However, if you're a good detective, you'll find evidence that Jews came to the New World as far back as the Spanish Inquisition. Some were even on board Columbus's ships. American shores have always been viewed as the land of freedom, opportunity, and religious liberty. Whenever and wherever problems arose for the Jews, many sought safety in America. Jews who have made the United States their home come from all over the world—Europe, South America, Asia, and the Middle East—and have brought the traditions of the "old country" with them.

"Mom, where's the candle?" Michael calls out.

"Look in the pantry," she suggests.

Sure enough, Michael finds one. He gets the rest of the Hide 'n Seek kit together: a medium-sized brown paper bag, and a feather to sweep the pieces of bread into the bag. Outside, darkness has settled in, and the street lamps are all aglow. Suddenly, he hears the garage door open. Dad and Jessica are home from her

piano lesson. "They're here," he calls out, rushing to the front door, kit in hand, ready to greet his father.

"I knew you'd be ready," his dad grins. He removes the candle from the kit and lights it, while Jessica turns off the lights. The candle flickers, lighting the way. "Give me a hint, Michael," his dad says.

"You're very cold," Michael responds.

Dad ponders the situation. His eyes catch something on the floor. He strides over to the other side of the room. "Hot, very hot, even hotter," Michael coaches him. Bending down, Dad sweeps the first chunk of bread into the brown bag.

Michael continues to guide him as he winds his way from room to room. Soon Dad has managed to collect all the chametz. He recites the traditional blessing and places the bag aside. "Tomorrow we'll burn the chametz on the barbecue, but first let's sweep up."

"I don't get it," Michael exclaims. "This year I went out of my way to find really good hiding places."

"Next year don't forget to clean up the trail of crumbs," Dad winks.

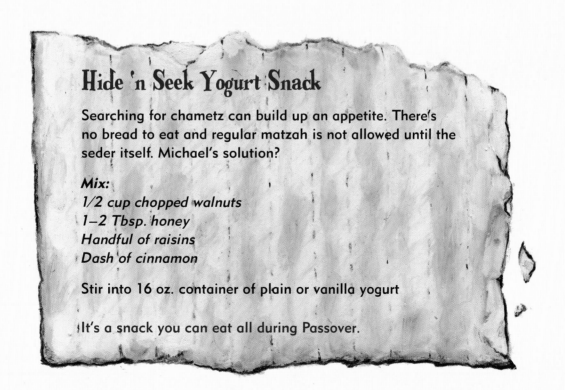

Hide 'n Seek Yogurt Snack

Searching for chametz can build up an appetite. There's no bread to eat and regular matzah is not allowed until the seder itself. Michael's solution?

Mix:
1/2 cup chopped walnuts
1–2 Tbsp. honey
Handful of raisins
Dash of cinnamon

Stir into 16 oz. container of plain or vanilla yogurt

It's a snack you can eat all during Passover.

Gibraltar
Preparing the Seder Plate

WHY IS A BRICK BEING USED TO MAKE CHAROSET?

When your parents cook a new dish and the texture doesn't come out right, they might say it's "thick as a brick." But can you imagine anyone actually eating a brick?

Meriam Pariente knows the answer. It's a secret she shares with her grandmother, Sarah Benady, who comes from Gibraltar. The Benadys first settled there in the 1730's. They have many unusual Passover customs that they've handed down from one generation to the next.

One of their traditions connects Sukkot with Passover. Every year, when Sukkot is over, Meriam helps her father wrap up the *lulav*—the long palm branch that symbolizes the harvest—as well as the *aravot* and *hadasim* (the willow and myrtle branches). They store them in a safe place, so that exactly six months later they can use them as fuel for baking matzah.

But what about the brick? Every year Meriam's grandmother reminds her how Pharaoh forced the Hebrew slaves to make bricks. "That's why we eat charoset," she explains. "It reminds us of the mortar the slaves used to lay the bricks." Meriam helps gather the ingredients for making Grandma Sarah's charoset recipe: dates, apples, nuts, almonds, bananas, wine, sugar, and cinnamon. Once the ingredients have been mixed to the right thickness, her grandmother says, "Go get the brick, please."

*G*ibraltar's Jewish community is a blend of Jews who fled from Spain and Portugal to England and Morocco and finally settled in Gibraltar, a peninsula on Spain's southern coast. The first Jews came in the 14th century. One hundred years later, all traces of Jewish life disappeared with the Spanish Inquisition. In 1704, Britain captured Gibraltar and in 1729, it signed an agreement with the Sultan of Morocco, permitting Jewish merchants to return to Gibraltar. Today, there are only six hundred Jews there, but all of its four original synagogues are still being used.

The first time her grandmother told her to do this, Meriam's eyes popped open wide as she watched Mrs. Benady break a few pieces off the brick and crush them into a powder. When her grandmother added the finely grated brick dust into the charoset. Meriam let out a gasp. Her grandmother held her close. "It's my secret ingredient for helping us remember how difficult a life our ancestors had."

The Missing Ingredient: Another Brick Story

What happens if you don't have the ingredients to make charoset? That's the question that a group of Jewish Union soldiers asked themselves during the Civil War. They were out in the wilderness of West Virginia, and they wanted to make a seder to celebrate Passover. They didn't seem to have any problem finding a bone, an egg, salt water, or even bitter herbs. But they couldn't obtain the ingredients for charoset. The solution? They put a real brick in its place on the seder plate. Little did they know that they were following a tradition of their fellow Jews on the distant peninsula of Gibraltar.

Charoset
Keeping in Step with the Rambam

Maimonides (Rambam) the great 12th century Jewish scholar, had his own recipe for Charoset.* It appears in the *Mishneh Torah*, his extensive commentary on the Talmud. His instructions call for stepping on the ingredients the same way one stomps on grapes to make wine:

"And how do you make Charoset? You take dates or dried figs, or raisins or something similar, tread on them and put vinegar on them, and spice them with spice like clay with straw, and bring it to the table on Passover eve."

* This recipe, provided by Dr. Susan Weingarten, is from her forthcoming book *Charoset: The Taste of History*.

Turkey
Reenacting the Story

WHY DOES THIS SEDER BEGIN WITH A PLAY?

"Knock, knock," giggles Albert Bechar.

"Who's there?" his twin sister Rebecca answers with a broad smile.

The two burst out in laughter, jumping up and down, shouting, "It's Padré's turn tonight." Padré is the Spanish word for "father." It is also the word for father in

Ladino, the Sephardic Jewish language based on Spanish with words from Hebrew, Turkish, French, Italian, and Arabic. In Turkey, where Albert and Rebecca live, Ladino is spoken within the family.

The twins have good reason to be excited. Their father has been chosen to act out the play at the beginning of tonight's seder. The Torah teaches that parents must tell their children the story of the Exodus from Egypt. To fulfill this commandment, the Bechar family chooses a different adult each year to put on a short skit before they begin reading from the Haggadah. This tradition is followed by many Jewish families in Turkey and other countries in the Sephardic world.

*J*ews have lived in Turkey—originally called Anatolia—ever since the 4th century B.C.E., where they had prosperous and active communities. Centuries later, when news of the Spanish expulsion reached the Ottoman Empire, its leader—Sultan Beyazit II—issued a decree welcoming the fleeing Jews to his shores. Ever since, the Ottoman Empire and the Turkish Republic have offered Jews a safe haven from persecution. Today, the majority of Turkey's Jews live in Istanbul. Most are Sephardim. There are also communities in Izmir, Ankara, Bursa, and Adana.

"Pssst," Albert whispers to his sister. Rebecca looks up and sees him pointing to a small, soft suitcase. They wink at each other knowingly. Padré's costume is inside, and a tall stick is resting against the wall next to it.

"Children, it's time to bathe and get dressed."

"Coming, Madré." They skip in the direction of their mother's voice. She's laid out new holiday clothing on their beds. Taking turns, they shower and dress. Soon they hear Padré entering the house.

"Shalom, shalom, is anyone home?" he calls out, sounding as though he is rehearsing for tonight's play. At Uncle Yizak and Aunt Rashel's home, they are greeted with warm hugs and kisses on both cheeks. Twenty family members sit around the seder table. Uncle Yizak sits at the head and Padré is next to him.

The seder begins. As Uncle Yizak is about to remove the middle matzah from the seder table, Rebecca catches Padré slipping out the front door. Uncle Yizak breaks the matzah and places the *afikomen* in a special napkin with a pocket. He passes it to the children.

"Remember to hide it well," he cautions, adding, "and now let's begin reading the Haggadah."

Suddenly, a loud knock is heard at the front door. Uncle Yizak is startled.

"Who could that be?" he asks. He gets up and opens the front door wide for all to see. It is a man wearing a long biblical robe tied at the waist. A flowing white cloth with a braided black rope circles his head. The man is holding a stick over his shoulder with a bundle tied to it.

"Where are you coming from?" asks Uncle Yizak.

"From the land of Egypt," answers the traveler.

Uncle Yizak acts surprised. "What, you're no longer a slave?" he exclaims.

"Now I am a free man," the visitor answers proudly.

"And where are you going?" persists Uncle Yizak.

With a broad smile, the man pauses before answering: "I am going to Jerusalem."

A burst of applause can be heard from the table. Everyone is so glad to hear this news. Happiest of all are Albert and Rebecca. They jump off their seats, run to the man, and lead him to the table. He tussles their hair.

"Good job," Albert whispers in his Padré's ear.

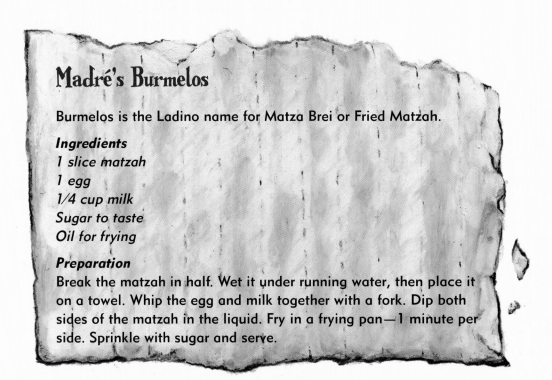

Madré's Burmelos

Burmelos is the Ladino name for Matza Brei or Fried Matzah.

Ingredients
1 slice matzah
1 egg
1/4 cup milk
Sugar to taste
Oil for frying

Preparation
Break the matzah in half. Wet it under running water, then place it on a towel. Whip the egg and milk together with a fork. Dip both sides of the matzah in the liquid. Fry in a frying pan—1 minute per side. Sprinkle with sugar and serve.

Ethiopia
The Passover Sacrifice

WHY IS THIS LAMB BEING SACRIFICED?

Aviva Aveira was four years old when she left Meraiva, her village in Ethiopia. She remembers the difficult journey she made on foot along with her family—first to Khartoum, Sudan, and then to an outlying desert area where planes took off for Israel.

The history of the Jews of Ethiopia remains a mystery. What is certain is that they have lived in this African country for thousands of years, residing in mountain villages near rivers and streams. While most were farmers, a few were craftsmen, working as tinsmiths and tailors. The Torah, which Ethiopian Jews call "Orit," served as the center of their lives, and they kept many of its traditions. From November 1984 until January 1985, eight thousand Ethiopian Jews were brought to Israel in a secret mission called Operation Moses. Later in 1985, Operation Joshua brought eight hundred more. The largest rescue—Operation Solomon—occurred on May 24, 1991, bringing another 14,324 Ethiopian Jews to Israel.

"I'm tired," she complained during the long ordeal.

Her grandfather understood. Hugging her close, he smiled. "This year we are finally going to Jerusalem."

Grandfather was a very old man. While they walked, he retold stories about Jerusalem that the Kess told every year at the Passover seder held in the village synagogue.

Every Jewish community in Ethiopia has a Kess—a great rabbi and leader. Aviva remembers the way her grandfather listened carefully to the instructions of the Kess, as he prepared for Passover. On the morning before the seder, her father, grandfather, and other village members brought a lamb to the Kess.

"This is the lamb that the Kess will sacrifice for the Passover meal, according to the laws of the Torah," they explained. "After he slaughters it, we will roast it. Tonight, in the synagogue, we will arrange the meat on a large tray in front of the Kess. Alongside of it will be a bowl of round matzot made by the village women. When the seder is over, we will burn any remaining meat, since we are not allowed to eat it tomorrow."

There were no Haggadahs in Ethiopia, no seder plates with maror, charoset, or egg. The Kess read the Passover story from the Torah, a large, thick book that looked nothing like a Torah scroll. This Torah was

not written in Hebrew but in *Ge'ez*, a holy language known only to the Kess.

Aviva remembers that last seder night in Ethiopia. The whole community gathered in the synagogue. The Kess sat at the front. Once he finished reading the story, members of the community appointed as servers gave each person a portion of the grilled lamb and a piece of matzah. They ate it while drinking *chilka*, a drink prepared from honey, water, a little salt, ground and blended sesame seeds, and *noog*, a brown variety of sesame seeds native to Ethiopia. Munching on the special Passover food, they listened to the Kess tell stories about Jerusalem. "Imagine what the homes look like in Jerusalem, imagine what the people do...what **we** will do in Jerusalem."

Aviva smiles. She no longer has to imagine what Jerusalem is like.

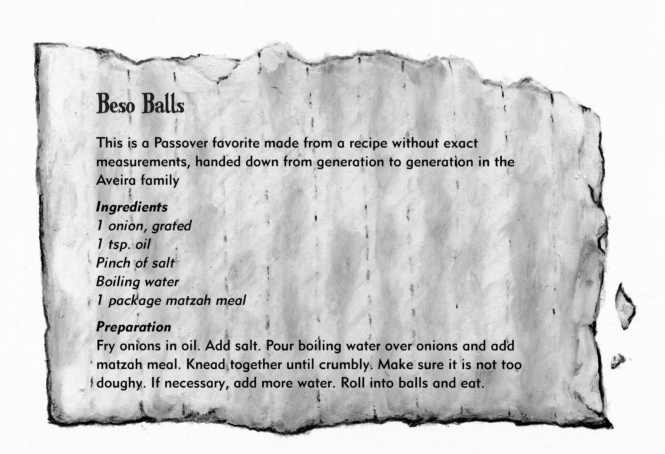

Beso Balls

This is a Passover favorite made from a recipe without exact measurements, handed down from generation to generation in the Aveira family

Ingredients
1 onion, grated
1 tsp. oil
Pinch of salt
Boiling water
1 package matzah meal

Preparation
Fry onions in oil. Add salt. Pour boiling water over onions and add matzah meal. Knead together until crumbly. Make sure it is not too doughy. If necessary, add more water. Roll into balls and eat.

India: Cochin
The Four Questions

WHAT IS DIFFERENT ABOUT THIS MAH NISHTANAH?

Imagine holding a silver seder plate, filled with all its symbolic foods, during the entire time you recite the Four Questions. That's exactly what Ovadya Roby has to do every year. Ovadya celebrates the seder at his grandparents' house, along with his parents and three older brothers. Ovadya's family comes from Cochin. His ancestors first arrived there four hundred years ago. Today, his family lives in Israel, continuing the centuries-old Passover traditions handed down from one generation to the next.

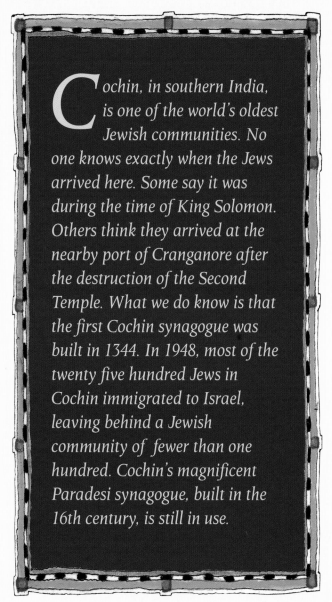

Cochin, in southern India, is one of the world's oldest Jewish communities. No one knows exactly when the Jews arrived here. Some say it was during the time of King Solomon. Others think they arrived at the nearby port of Cranganore after the destruction of the Second Temple. What we do know is that the first Cochin synagogue was built in 1344. In 1948, most of the twenty five hundred Jews in Cochin immigrated to Israel, leaving behind a Jewish community of fewer than one hundred. Cochin's magnificent Paradesi synagogue, built in the 16th century, is still in use.

Ovadya loves helping his grandmother Rachel set the table. Cochin Jews like silver. Each guest gets a small silver kiddush cup on its own silver plate. The seder plate is a large silver tray that sits on a silver or brass stand. Three covered silver boxes are placed in the middle of the tray. One is for charoset; the second is for vinegar used for dipping the maror; and the third is for wine. The maror, karpas, shankbone, and egg are placed around the boxes. Three small, thick *matzah shmurah* (guarded matzah) are placed on top of the silver boxes. Everyone from Cochin knows that the top matzah stands for the Kohanim (the priestly class in ancient Israel). It has two lines like this | | marked on it. The middle matzah has three lines | | | for the Levites. The bottom matzah has four lines | | | | for the Israelites. The entire tray is covered with a shiny opaque cloth embroidered with gold threads.

When the seder tray is set, Ovadya and his grandmother take twelve pieces of matzah—to symbolize the twelve tribes of Israel—and place them on the table, around the tray.

After the kiddush is recited, everyone in the family helps remove the twelve pieces of matzah before they begin reading from the Haggadah. With the matzah removed, they are now able to hold on to the tray and recite together, "*Ha lachmah anya,*" (This is the bread of our suffering) the section explaining why we eat matzah. Then, as a group, they lift the tray off the table, holding on to its stand for a few seconds. They reread this section three times, lifting the plate each time, to emphasize the message.

Then the seder plate is put back on the table to rest for a few minutes before Ovadya picks it up to recite the *Mah Nishtanah*. It's heavy and hard for Ovadya to hold. His father helps him. Ovadya can hardly wait till he's a few years older, when he'll be bigger and stronger, and able to hold the tray on his own.

Grandma Rachel Roby's Charoset

Ovadya's Grandma Rachel starts making her charoset the day after Purim. It takes her two days to make this special recipe. When she's finished she bottles and covers it, placing it in a room where there is no hametz. It stands there for a month in order to have the right consistency for the seder night. Here's how she makes it:

Ingredients
2 pounds pitted dates
Chopped walnuts

Place 2 pounds of pitted dates into a pot with enough water to cover. Cover the pot and boil the dates until they get pulpy. Let them cool overnight. The next day, squeeze out the juice from each date and put it into another pot. Cover the pot and bring the juice to a boil on a high flame. Remove the lid and continue boiling for 4 to 5 hours, until the water evaporates and the juice becomes syrupy. Cool the syrup, then bottle and cover it. When the seder night arrives, mix the date syrup with chopped walnuts and serve.

Israel: Kibbutz Shamir

Maggid

WHY IS THERE A STAGE FOR THIS SEDER?

Noa Avishai is not at all nervous about singing the *Mah Nishtanah* in front of the seven hundred people who will be at her seder. After all, at Kibbutz Shamir everybody is part of one big family.

"Hurry, Noa," calls her friend Liat, "it's time for the last rehearsal in the dining hall."

Noa won't be singing the Four Questions alone. She's part of a choir. Nine other friends will be on the stage singing with her. Uriel, the kibbutz member in charge of the dining room, is their choir leader. He will accompany them on the piano, and Mark, a student at the local college, will play the guitar. This is the first time Noa and Liat are going to perform at the seder, and they are very excited.

The first kibbutz was established in the 1880s as a collective farm community, long before the State of Israel came into being. Kibbutzim played an important role in Israel's development and helped make the country famous for its fruits and vegetables. Kibbutz Shamir was founded in November 1935, by pioneers from the Shomer Ha'Tzair (Young Guardians) movement in Romania. It is in the northwestern part of the Upper Galilee. Kibbutz Shamir has a population of 630. Like other kibbutzim, it makes its money from industry in addition to agriculture.

A kibbutz seder is like a school play. In addition to the choir and a dance group, more than thirty-five different kibbutz members will lead the seder this year. Each will take a turn reading from the special Haggadah put out by the kibbutz movement. It is different from other Haggadahs printed around the world. It begins with special prayers celebrating spring, the season of Passover. Then it combines traditional Haggadah texts, portions of the Bible describing the Exodus, with poetry written by Israel's most famous poet—Chaim Nachman Bialik.

"Girls, please get up on the stage," Uriel calls to them. He hands out sheets of paper. "Don't hold these in front of your face. We want to see you sing," he reminds them.

Even the kibbutz version of the *Mah Nishtanah* is different. See if you can recognize the changes:

Why is this night different from all other nights?
On all other nights we eat either chametz or matzah.
On this night we eat only matzah.

On all other nights we eat either sitting or reclining.
Tonight we all recline.

On all other nights we eat a quick meal.
Tonight the meal is longer and it's a night for staying awake.

On all other nights we talk about things in general.
On this night we talk about the exodus from Egypt.

When the rehearsal is over, Liat tugs at Noa's blouse. "Let's go see what Dina, the chief cook, is preparing in the kitchen. Maybe we can help her with the *kneidels* (matzah balls)." Noa's mouth begins to water. There's nothing like Dina's kneidels in chicken soup!

"OK," she agrees, grabbing Liat's hand. The two run to the kitchen.

Dina Ben-Efraim's Kneidels

Ingredients
1 cup matzah meal
3 Tbsp. oil
1 tsp. salt
4 Tbsp. parsley (optional)
Pepper to taste
2 cups boiling water
2 eggs
Chicken soup

Preparation
Put the matzah meal, oil, salt and parsley into a bowl. Add pepper to taste and mix. Pour in the hot water and mix with a wooden spoon. Add eggs and mix. If the mix is too thin, add more matzah meal. Moisten hands and roll dough into small balls. Simmer the matzah balls for a half-hour in a covered pot of boiling chicken soup. Cover the pot when the matzah balls come to the top.

Caspian
Sea

TURKMENISTAN

IRAQ

AFGHANISTAN

★ Tehran

IRAN

★
Baghdad

• Shiraz

N

Persian Gulf

SAUDI
ARABIA

Iran
Dayenu

WHY ARE THERE SCALLIONS AT THIS SEDER TABLE?

Danny Somechiyan loves to listen to his father tell stories about leaving Iran.
They remind him of the Exodus from Egypt.

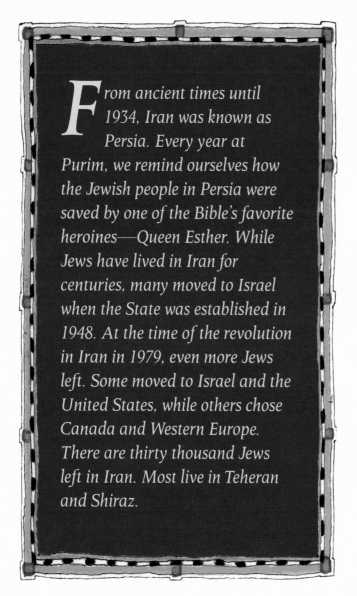

From ancient times until 1934, Iran was known as Persia. Every year at Purim, we remind ourselves how the Jewish people in Persia were saved by one of the Bible's favorite heroines—Queen Esther. While Jews have lived in Iran for centuries, many moved to Israel when the State was established in 1948. At the time of the revolution in Iran in 1979, even more Jews left. Some moved to Israel and the United States, while others chose Canada and Western Europe. There are thirty thousand Jews left in Iran. Most live in Teheran and Shiraz.

"We were like the Hebrew slaves — leaving in a hurry," his father explains. "We didn't have a leader like Moses to tell us what to do. We just had to grab the opportunity and go, leaving everything behind—our beautiful homes, family and friends, businesses, everything we owned, even our family photos. Now the pictures and memories are all up here," he says, pointing to his forehead.

Danny often wonders what it would be like living in Iran. He knows that he still celebrates Passover exactly the way his grandparents did, even though he lives in Israel.

The day after Purim, his mother starts cleaning the house— beginning with the kitchen cupboards and the dishes. The first time he saw his mother put a small stone into a big pot of boiling water, he was a little boy of four.

"What are you doing?" Danny asked.

"I'm following the tradition of your *maman bozorg* (grandmother)," she answered. "I'm going to dip all my cooking pots in here, say a special prayer, and then I'll use them to prepare our Passover meals."

Danny thought that was a strange thing to do.

Things got even stranger when he saw his mother set the table for the seder. He had learned all about the seder plate in school, but he had never heard about using scallions.

"Why are you putting out onions?" he asked.

"Just wait and see," his mother smiled. "This year you're old enough to stay awake and enjoy a real Farsi (Persian) seder."

That night, family and friends from Iran sat down at the seder table. Danny sat next to his cousin Eyal. Right before singing *Dayenu*, Danny's mother passed around the scallions.

"Take one," Eyal insisted, handing him the bowl. Shrugging, Danny took a green onion and sang along with everyone:

"Had God rescued us from Egypt and not punished the Egyptians, dayenu."

Suddenly, Danny felt something hit him on the shoulder. He turned to look at his cousin, who was already singing the second line:

"Had God passed judgment on them and not on their idols, dayenu."

This time Danny saw Eyal lift his right hand and hit him on the shoulder with the scallion.

"Hey, what do you think you're doing?" he yelled. A giggle could be heard around the table, but the singing continued:

"Had God destroyed their idols, but not killed their firstborn, dayenu."

Again, Eyal lifted his hand.

"You're not going to hit me again!" shouted Danny, this time raising his scallion in Eyal's direction. Now everyone was laughing and clapping.

"It is our tradition to take a scallion and lightly hit the shoulder of the person sitting to our right," Danny's mother explained. "*Ameh* (Aunt) Soraya is sitting there. Why don't you take your scallion and lightly slap it on her shoulder?" Ameh Soraya gave him a nod that meant, "It's OK."

"But why?" he asked.

"What were the Jews in Egypt?" his mother asked.

"Slaves," Danny answered.

"And if they didn't work hard enough, what did the Egyptians do?"

"They hit the Jews with a whip."

"Exactly. We use the scallions to remind us."

Danny brushed Ameh Sorayah's shoulder with his scallion but thought that hitting Eyal back would have been a lot more fun.

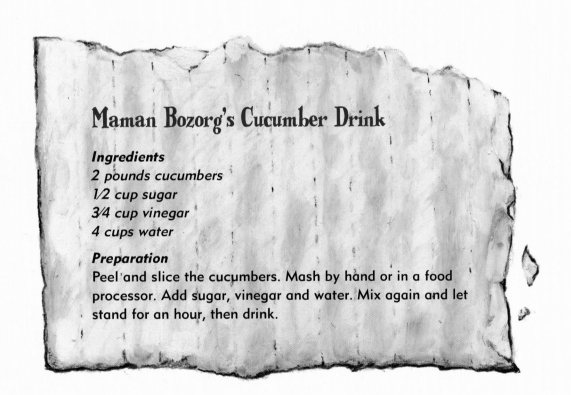

Maman Bozorg's Cucumber Drink

Ingredients
2 pounds cucumbers
1/2 cup sugar
3/4 cup vinegar
4 cups water

Preparation
Peel and slice the cucumbers. Mash by hand or in a food processor. Add sugar, vinegar and water. Mix again and let stand for an hour, then drink.

Morocco
Mimouna

WHY DO WE HAVE A FEAST WHEN PASSOVER ENDS?

It's the last day of Passover, and Hodaya Peretz can't wait to put on the shiny, long green caftan with gold embroidery that her *savta* and *saba* (grandmother and grandfather) brought back from their trip to Morocco. Savta Mazal bought identical caftans for herself and Hodaya's mother, Lilach. Tonight the three will wear them at the Mimouna celebration held in her grandparents' house.

The Peretz family left Morocco for Israel in 1955. The family has grown, with hundreds of relatives living throughout Israel, from Kiryat Shmona in the north to Eilat in the south.

During the weekdays following the seder, the women in Hodaya's family prepared for the Mimouna. They made a rainbow of sweets: colorful, swirly, cone-shaped cookies made from whipped egg whites; cakes made from coconut, almonds, and chocolate; candied fruits and carrots; dried fruits; and jellies made with raisins, walnuts, kumquats, and nuts. Hodaya had fun helping Savta Mazal prepare the stuffed dates with walnuts. But her favorite sweet is marzipan, made from almond paste, and she loved watching her cousin Annette make teeny marzipan roses, bananas, strawberries, and peaches. When she grows up, Hodaya wants to become a marzipan artist like Annette.

Jews have lived in Morocco for more than two thousand years—ever since Nebuchadnezzar destroyed Jerusalem. Moroccan Jewish traditions are a colorful blend of Oriental, Berber, Arab, and Spanish customs, reflecting the history of that country. Jews began leaving Morocco for Israel when the State was established in 1948. From 1955 to 1957, more than seventy thousand Moroccan Jews emigrated. In 1961, Moroccan King Hassan II gave the Jews the right to leave. In addition to Israel, many went to France, Great Britain, the United States, and Canada. There are only five thousand Jews left in Morocco.

Savta Mazal looks at her watch. Passover is about to end, and it's time to set the Mimouna table. Hodaya's grandfather places a fresh fish, surrounded by lettuce and wrapped in cellophane, on a table outside the entrance of the house. The fish symbolizes fertility, which is important to Moroccan Jews.

"Hodaya, come help bring out the sweets," Savta bids her. Hodaya brings out one plate of goodies after the next. Her mouth waters. So many good things to eat.

"Why do only Moroccan Jews have a Mimouna?" she asks her mother.

"There are several answers given," her mother answers, "but I like the one that is connected to Maimonides, the famous Jewish physician and Bible scholar who lived in the Middle Ages. He was born in Spain but later moved to Morocco. Legend has it that he was born on Passover eve and circumcised on the last day of the holiday. The Mimouna is a celebration of his *Brit Milah*."

The guests begin to arrive, but they don't stay very long. They go from house to house, sampling everyone's festive dishes.

"I'm not sure about Maimonides," Hodaya grins. "I think the Mimouna is just an excuse to go to lots of parties."

Savta Mazal's Stuffed Dates

Ingredients
Dates
Walnuts
Powdered sugar

Cut dates in half and remove the pits. Break walnuts in half and fill each half date with two or three walnut pieces. Roll the stuffed dates in powdered sugar. Serve the dates in small candy cups.

Passover Potpourri

WHY DOES THIS HOLIDAY HAVE SO MANY DIFFERENT CUSTOMS?

From the time of the destruction of the Second Temple almost two thousand years ago, until 1948, the Jews were a nation without a country. By living in all corners of the world, the Jewish people developed a variety of Passover customs, often adopting them from their host cultures. Let's take a peek at a few more traditions.

Egypt

Believe it or not, Jews still live in Egypt. The numbers are few, as most left the country once the State of Israel was established. Regardless of where they are living, many Egyptian Jews still follow the practice of tying a piece of matzah in a napkin sack. When they read the section *Ha Lachma Anya* (this is the bread of affliction) they pass the sack around the table. As each person receives the sack, that person places it on the right shoulder. The seder leader asks: "Where are you from?" The person answers "Egypt." The leader continues, "Where are you going?" Switching the sack to the left shoulder, the person answers: "Jerusalem."

Europe

Ashkenazi Jews, those of European descent, share many of the same Passover customs. One ritual they all observe is dipping their pinky fingers into their glasses of wine while reciting the Ten Plagues. They let the droplets fall on their plates. This is to emphasize that even the Egyptians were God's creatures, and the Egyptians' suffering should diminish our joy.

Hungary

There is a custom among some Jews in this central European country to decorate the seder table with gold and silver jewelry to recall the items of precious metal that the Egyptians gave the Israelites before the tenth plague.

Morocco

Moroccan Jews have several colorful traditions. At the beginning of the seder, the leader lifts the seder tray and carries it from person to person, holding it over each one's head, declaring that the person is now free. Another interesting custom deals with Elijah. While Ashkenazi Jews welcome Elijah with a cup of wine placed on the table, some Jews in Casablanca place a large ornamented chair with brocaded pillows near the seder table to await the prophet's arrival.

Ger

Ger is the Yiddish name of Góra Kalwaria, a small town in Poland. Gerer Hasidim are the Ultra-Orthodox dynasty originating from this village. The Gerer Rebbe and his followers live in Jerusalem. For this group, acting out the Passover story does not begin and end with the seder night. Tradition has it that Moses and the Children of Israel left Egypt and crossed the Sea of Reeds on the seventh night of Passover. The Gerer Hasidim observe this event by gathering in their *shtibel* (small synagogue) on the seventh night, where they celebrate the crossing of the sea by drinking wine, dancing, and pouring a barrel of water on the floor. Then they lift up their long coats and walk through the water, calling out the different names of towns that are on the way to Ger.

Crypto Jews

Sephardi Jews are those whose ancestors fled Spain and Portugal around the Inquisition. Many converted to avoid persecution, yet continued to observe Jewish traditions. There is evidence that some Hispanics in Texas and Mexico, who are practicing Christians, are descended from these *Crypto* (hidden) Jews. During the period of Lent, which falls around Passover, it is a custom for some of these Christians to eat *Pan de Semita*, which means "Semitic Bread." It is made by combining two cups of flour with half a cup of water, and a few tablespoons of butter or olive oil. The ingredients are mixed and baked, resulting in a flat, unleavened bread.

More Recipes

Yummy Mashed Potato Kugel

Ingredients
5 large potatoes
2 medium onions
Handful of parsley
Dash of paprika

Preparation
1. Wash the potatoes and boil them until soft.
2. Peel the onions and chop into small pieces. Sauté until golden brown.
3. Chop the parsley and add to onions.
4. Remove potatoes from the stove, cool, peel, and mash.
5. Add the sautéed onions and parsley, and mix well.
6. Place the mixture in a greased oven-proof dish. Sprinkle with paprika.
7. Cover and bake at 350° for 20 minutes. Uncover and bake for another 10 minutes. Serve hot.

Serves 4 to 6

Good Morning Matzah Brie

Ingredients
2 pieces of matzah
1/2 cup milk
2 Tbsp. margarine
1/4 cup sugar mixed with 1 tsp. cinnamon

Preparation
1. Pour the milk into a shallow bowl. Break the matzah into large pieces and soak them in the milk.
2. Melt the margarine in a frying pan. Add the matzah. Sprinkle with the cinnamon mixture and fry for a minute. Turn the matzah over and sprinkle again with the mixture. Fry for another minute. Serve hot.
Serves 2

French Cauliflower Soup

Ingredients
1 large cauliflower
1 large potato
2 large onions
2 garlic cloves
5 cups boiling water
2 tsp. powdered chicken soup
3/4 cup white wine

Preparation
1. Peel and chop the onions and garlic. Sauté them in a large pot until golden brown.
2. Peel the potato, cut into pieces, and add to pot.
3. Wash and separate the cauliflower into florets and add to pot.
4. Dissolve the powdered soup in the boiling water and add to the pot.
5. Add the wine
6. Bring to a boil, then lower to medium heat and cook for an hour or until the potato pieces and cauliflower florets are soft.
7. Cool. Mash the mixture in the pot (or puree in blender) until fairly smooth. Reheat to serve.

Serves 4 to 6

Granny Fanny's Cold Egg Soup

Ingredients
6 hard-boiled eggs
3 cups cold water
Salt to taste

Preparation
1. Peel the eggs, cut them into pieces, and place them in a bowl.
2. Add the water and stir until the water turns yellow.
3. Add salt to taste.
Refrigerate. Serve cold.

Serves 6

Glossary

All words translated from Hebrew unless otherwise noted

Afikomen — matzah hidden at the seder to capture the attention of children

Beitzah — egg; placed on seder plate as a symbol of spring and to recall Passover sacrifice

Brit Milah — circumcision

Chametz — leavened grains not permitted on Passover

Charoset — mixture of chopped apples and nuts to recall mortar Israelite slaves used in Egypt

Chazeret — optional second bitter herb on some seder plates

Dayenu — literally "it would have been enough"; name of song sung at Passover seder

Elijah — Biblical prophet said to visit each seder

Ge'ez — Holy language of Ethiopian Jews

Haggadah — literally "to tell"; book of prayers, psalms, rituals and text used at the seder

Halachma Anya — literally "the bread of poverty" (Aramaic); a prayer recited at the seder

Hasidim — an ultra-Orthodox branch of Judaism founded in 18th century Europe

Karpas — green vegetable eaten at the seder to symbolize spring

Kess — religious leader of an Ethiopian Jewish community (Amharic)

Kibbutz (pl. kibbutzim) — communal settlement in Israel

Kiddush – prayer over wine recited on Shabbat and Jewish holidays

Kneidel — dumpling (Yiddish)

Kohanim — those descended from the priests of the Holy Temple

Ladino — a Judeo-Spanish language spoken by Sephardic Jews descended from those who left Spain during the Inquisition

Levites — descendants of the tribe of Levi who assisted the priests in the Holy Temple

Lulav — palm branch bound with aravot (willows) and hadasim (myrtle), used on the Jewish holiday of Sukkot

Maman Bozorg — grandmother (Farsi)

Maror — bitter herb eaten at seder

Matzah (pl. matzot) — unleavened bread eaten on Passover

Mimouna — festival celebrated by Moroccan Jews at the end of Passover

Maimonides — 13th century Jewish philosopher

Mah Nishtanah — literally "what is different," opening line of Four Questions asked by youngest child at seder

Matzah Shmurah — literally "guarded matzah"; matzah prepared from grain that is watched from the time of harvesting through baking to insure that it doesn't come into contact with moisture

Passover — Jewish holiday that commemorates the Exodus from Egypt

Pan de Semita — literally "semitic bread" (Spanish); refers to matzah

Purim — Jewish holiday that commemorates the victory over the villain Haman in Shushan, Persia, as recounted in the Biblical book of Esther

Saba — grandfather

Savta — grandmother

Seder — literally "order"; the communal meal at which the story of the Exodus is retold and ritual foods are eaten

Seder Plate — plate containing the ritual foods eaten at the seder

Shomer Hatza'ir — pioneering youth movement that founded kibbutzim in Israel

Shtibel — literally "little home" (Yiddish); refers to small synagogue

Sukkot — Jewish holiday that celebrates the fall harvest

Sephardim — Jews descended from those who lived on the Iberian peninsula

Shalom — Hebrew word for "hello," "good-bye," and "peace"

Torah — scroll containing first Five Books of Moses in Bible

Zero'a — bone placed on seder plate to recall the first Passover sacrifice in Egypt

About the Author

Tami Lehman-Wilzig is the author of several children's books including *Tasty Bible Stories* and *Keeping the Promise*: *A Torah's Journey*, an International Reading Association's Teacher's Choice Award winner. She lives in Petach Tikvah, Israel.

About the Illustrator

Elizabeth Wolf has a BFA from the University of Michigan. She is a cartographic designer and mapmaker and an illustrator of more than 40 books. An award-winning mosaic tile artist and mural painter, she lives in Boise, ID.